A Tower of Faith
in the
Heart of the City

1888 - 1988

A Tower of Faith in the Heart of the City

1888 - 1988

Centennial History of the First Congregational Church of Long Beach, California

Hope Publishing House
P. O. Box 60008
Pasadena, CA 91116

Copyright © 1988 by
Hope Publishing House
P. O. Box 60008
Pasadena, CA 91116

Printed in the U.S.A.

Manuscript Editor: Faith Annette Sand

ISBN 0-932727-22-0 hardcover

Jotham Bixby

Table of Contents

Acknowledgements

Special thanks is due to the Centennial Committee which was chaired by Nancy Merritt. This committee included Harold Judson, Scott Ramsay, Ernest Fowler, Mary Becker, Helene Kennan, Aileen Lovett, Ethel Furboter, Irma Baldwin, Virginia Ossen, Nan Nutt and Marion Hinze. It was through their dedicated energy this project was made possible.

Grateful thanks are also due to the myriad people who made written contributions or were interviewed in order to furnish the data needed to compile this text. They include: Emerson G. Hangen, Scott Ramsay, Ernest M. Fowler, Nancy Merritt, Myfanway and Harold Judson, John and Billie Pownall, Eva and Duane George, Glover Lawry, Mary Becker, Ernie Frank, Della and Spicer Ramsay, Leona H. Booth, Dorothy Baker, Doris Thomas, Anna Mae Webber, Fannie Belle Bellows, Helen Clark, Joan Smith, Helen M. Thomas, Virginia Ossen, Raezella and Stuart LeRoy Anderson, Diane and David Reed, Bruce V. Talbert, Shelby J. Light, Win Gould, Dwight Hoelscher, Henry R. Rust and Mary Ellen Kilsby.

Introduction

For a church in California, a hundredth anniversary is not only a major event, it is rare enough to be notable. Pulling the various strands of a church's life and weaving them together to produce a historical picture to mark the centennial is a fascinating exercise and challenge. What contributed to a vigorous and well-supported worship life? outreach activities? a superior education program? What were the less obvious factors and associations that made the church run smoothly? ...the choir program? ...those groups who are often not mentioned in annual reports or in brief histories because of the supportive role they played?

It has been said, "Without a past we have no future." A centennial celebration is a natural time to take stock of the past. This is a church with a great history, a splendid sanctuary and building, and a dedicated, committed congregation.

Those who preceded me in this office watched Long Beach grow into a major metropolitan center. They helped facilitate the building of a great sanctuary and a fine organ, two housing projects to meet the needs of the elderly and those with handicapping conditions, and an educational facility which no longer stands. Programs to meet the needs of the changing community have been implemented. Today, the Saturday and Summer Program for Children and Youth continues while English as a Second Language classes have been added.

People have become a church community and the third generation of an amazing number of families are now taking their place in the leadership of this congregation. Marriages and baptisms, memorial services and emergency sessions in the pastor's office mark the life of a church family as Sunday after Sunday, week after week, lives are enriched, minds are stretched, hearts are made larger, tears are cherished and laughter is shared.

We do so appreciate Faith Annette Sand, our editor, who took enormous amounts of time to talk with many of our members and worked lovingly and graciously with our Centennial Committee. We owe special thanks to Diane Reed who, along with Scott Ramsay and Ernest Fowler, moved the project through mid-1986, and to Dr. Emerson G. Hangen whose writing of our early history served as the background of this tapestry. As we stand back and look at this we are reminded how God's hand has been part of the weaving, and we can see how God has protected us throughout.

I feel deeply privileged to have been called to the pastorate of First Congregational Church Long Beach in its 100th year. Few have missed the quite remarkable fact that this minister is a woman, indicative of the changes of the past and a harbinger of the rapid, dramatic changes that are yet to come.

It is my very great privilege now to be a part of all of this as we look forward into the second 100 years and into the twenty-first century. From Margaret and Jotham's pioneering beginning, the changes have been enormous, but they are relatively comfortable when compared to the dramatic changes pundits see ahead.

Excitement is in the air. You can feel the anticipation, and First Congregational Church of Long Beach, now "retrofitted by the Spirit," is ready to move into the next 100 years with inspiring worship, with ties that bind us into a family and with commitment to meet the needs of our community and our world as the Body of Christ.

My prayer is that we will have obedient hearts and be ready to follow the Spirit's leading into this new century of our worshiping together in the heart of the city. Amen.

— Dr. Mary Ellen Kilsby

1.

Beginnings in a Village Hamlet

The annals of church history in California remind us that, historically speaking, this part of the country is still in its youth. Unlike the venerable history of the Atlantic seaboard and New England where church history is recorded in centuries, here one speaks of decades.

The year 1620 marked the arrival of the Pilgrims in New England and with them the establishment of Congregationalism in the New World. Compared to that record, it is rather startling to learn that the three oldest Congregational churches in Southern California—Los Angeles First, Santa Barbara and San Bernardino—were established almost 250 years later in 1867. In the 1870s only one additional Congregational church was founded — the first Congregational Church in Riverside. As late as 1885 there were only eleven Congregational churches in all of Southern California.

But that year marked the beginning of a surge of new church growth. During the next five years, 26 Congregational churches were founded in this area. During this period of church expansion and enterprise the First Congregational Church of Long Beach came into being.

The City of Long Beach was at the beginning of its history in the latter part of the 1880s. Originally it developed because it had been chosen as a camp meeting site by the Methodists. Naturally the first church in the city was Methodist, started in 1887.

The first recorded mention of the Congregational Church in Long Beach occurs in the *Clerk's Record of Church Meetings,* dated January 25, 1888. Twelve people met to consider the "formation of a Congregational Church at Long Beach" at the invitation extended to those in the congregation who had met the previous Sunday in Cerritos Hall, located at the corner of Third Street and Cedar Avenue.

Such a meeting obviously did not occur spontaneously. While no prior official records are extant, we do know that the previous year, through the efforts of Mr. and Mrs. Jotham Bixby of Long Beach, a minister from Los Angeles — the Reverend A. M. Wells — came to town to establish a Congregational church.

The Bixbys were lifelong Congregationalist and Mrs. Margaret Bixby, as a charter member, had been instrumental in establishing the First Congregational Church of Los Angeles. By 1888 the Bixbys had built and owned the Cerritos Hall, at the time the only public building in Long Beach, which as such was much in demand for temperance rallies and religious meetings in this small, seaside resort of Long Beach.

Records indicate that by 1890 the town's population reached 564. In spite of the presence of the Methodist church in this small village, the annals list Revered Mr. Wells as a "missionary to this hamlet from the First Congregational Church of Los Angeles."

During his first year of mission endeavor, Mr. Wells followed the usual procedure, calling on homes, getting acquainted with people, trying to interest them in the new church he was commissioned to start. Mr. and Mrs. Bixby, whose names are practically synonymous with the founding of Long Beach, became the patron saints of the developing church. To give this new enterprise encouragement, they gave the use of Cerritos Hall for worship services. South of the hall a parsonage was built for the minister and his family.

Thus the road was paved for the historic meeting on January 25, 1888 in which a committee of five people was appointed to "frame and submit a statement of faith and covenant" for the proposed church and be ready to make a report at a future called meeting. Twelve days later a congregational meeting heard the committee's report — a statement of doctrine and a covenant for the admission of members, which is remarkably modern in tone and spirit. In part it said:

Christianity is a spirit and a life. It cannot therefore be expressed philosophically in a creed.... Christianity is the religion of daily life and is to be applied to all human affairs... We believe that the Scriptures constitute a continuing unfolding revelation of God which the discoveries of science, the facts of history and the providences of life are to aid us to interpret constantly and freshly.

In view of the rigid orthodoxy and sensitivity to theological formality of those days, such a statement demonstrated a liberal point of view — which has been a hallmark of this church throughout its history.

This report was adopted and another committee was appointed to forge a set of bylaws. Three days later the bylaws were also adopted by the congregation and the church was now officially organized. At the February 12, 1988 worship service 26 people were formally received into fellowship — eighteen by transfer of letter from other churches and eight by confession of faith. At the same time a slate of officers was elected to carry on the work of the new church and the members chose the name: The First Congregational Church of Long Beach, California. Articles of incorporation were drawn up and adopted on the 21st of March and were duly certified by the county clerk in Los Angeles and filed with the secretary of state of California. These articles of incorporation have served the church throughout its history and they are still operative today.

The final step to complete the church's organization was its reception into the fellowship of the Los Angeles Association of Congregational Churches. An official meeting of the association was held March 14 at the Long Beach church. In attendance were representatives from the churches in Los Angeles, East Los Angeles, Pasadena, Sierra Madre, Monrovia, Pomona, Riverside, Vernon and Westminster — reflecting how many Congregational churches already were organized by this date. Some questions were raised at the association meeting concerning the new church's "progressive" statement of faith. Considerable debate ensued, but the matter was ironed out in committee meetings. On April 3, a regular meeting of the association gathered in Los Angeles and the First Church of Long Beach was officially received into the fellowship.

This formal recognition and acceptance completed the missionary task of Reverend A. J. Wells. Now he could return to Los Angeles leaving the Long Beach church in a position to call a permanent pastor. At an official meeting on April 15 the congregation voted to extend a call to the Reverend R. M. Webster with the understanding that he would begin his duties May 1.

Under Mr. Webster's leadership the church prospered. He observed in his first report to the annual meeting, January 1889, that although the total membership of the church was only 31, the average attendance at Sunday worship services was 100. These were hard days for everyone. An economic depression not only made people hesitate joining the church, but the church's income was substantially reduced.

A year later with no economic recovery in sight, the minister voluntarily offered to reduce his salary from $125 per month to $100 per month. This offer was regretfully accepted by the church. The depression continued to make an adverse influence on the church, but Mr. Webster bravely stayed with the congregation through the difficult years. Finally after more than four years of dedicated leadership he submitted his resignation on October 23, 1893. It was reluctantly accepted by the church.

The next year Reverend Sidney C. Kendall was called to minister at the church. During his pastorate, just ten years after the church was founded, Mr. and Mrs. Jotham Bixby presented Cerritos Hall and the adjoining land to the church as a gift. These two pioneers of Long Beach had continued their generous support throughout the years and now capped their loyalty to the church with this munificent gift. Shortly thereafter, at the January 1899 annual meeting, Mr. Kendall resigned as pastor and a pastoral committee was appointed to search for a new minister.

In April the committee presented the recommendation that the Reverend Charles Pease be called, and the congregation concurred. Mr. Pease immediately and vigorously assumed his duties and under his leadership the church grew to such an extent that it became apparent Cerritos Hall would no longer accommodate their worship needs.

In 1901 at a regular meeting of the trustees a motion was adopted to undertake constructing a new church building. Plans presented by an architect were accepted and appointed committees were invested with the responsibility of carrying through the building of the second church structure on the present site of Third and Cedar.

As the growth rate continued to escalate, the church recognized a need to further define its membership. At a regular business meeting on April 17, 1901 the church adopted a set of *Regulations as to Membership in the First Congregational Church of Long Beach, California*. The preamble of that document demonstrates why the church was characterized as having a liberal orientation from its very early days.

This church belongs to that honorable body of Christians who are known as Congregationalists. The name implies simply this: that each Congregation is an independent organization, determining its own creed and governing itself in all matters practical and spiritual.

Congregationalism as a whole therefore acknowledges no creed which is binding in any sense upon the individual churches of that name. We, however, gladly and proudly acknowledge the magnificent history of Congregationalism, and receive the body of doctrine handed down from former times as a testimony to our [forebearers'] faith, and an evidence of the degree of truth to which they attained. Likewise the statement of doctrines upon which this particular church was founded we look upon as a milestone on the way of truth — to serve as a guide to better things, rather than the goal of our journeyings.

The Master taught that Truth is Life. Creeds are therefore an attempt to put life into language. They are ever imperfect and must give way to larger knowledge and better expression. Since [people] see truth from their own individual standpoint, we have no right to impose a creed, however short, as a test of membership in the Church of Christ. We desire this church to win the fellowship of all sincere seekers after life and truth, and are willing to allow to all the freedom we ask for ourselves in the interpretation of religion. As a church standing in the line of an historic faith we hold to all that is vital in its belief and teaching, but impose no creed and define no philosophy of faith for any who may desire to unite with us upon the basis of the Christ character and spirit.

The new church building was completed and dedicated on October 12, 1902 and worship services began to be conducted in it. At the January 4, 1904 annual meeting, the treasurer reported that the two notes of $4,500 and $900 had been paid off, making the church debt free. The trustees, who had negotiated a bank loan to pay for the new structure, were elated!

A note-burning ceremony brightened that meeting and the church could now move ahead, freed from building-incurred liabilities. Although the records that come down to us from those days have no hint of any problems faced by the church, there seemed to be financial difficulties from time to time. However, these were always surmounted and the church forged ahead under capable pastoral leadership.

Everything was going well.

2.

Time of Crisis

The first indication of dissension in the church records is a brief reference regarding a letter of membership transfer granted to Miss Ruth Cree on April 12, 1904 who moved her membership to Plymouth Congregational Church of Long Beach, a congregational church which had originated as an offshoot of First Church.

The records indicate that considerable dissatisfaction regarding theological matters had sprung up among some members of the church. However these people continued their relationship to First Church until the day after the annual meeting of 1904 when a group of the disgruntled members—which included "19 heads of families"—met and the unrest which had been implicit became explicit.

One matter discussed was how few of the Congregational people coming to Long Beach found themselves at home in First Church. New residents tended either to join other churches or formed no affiliation at all. In view of this situation, the possibility of forming a new Congregational church in Long Beach was advanced and "careful and prayerful consideration of what *ought* to be done occupied the entire evening."

Finally it was agreed that before any drastic steps were taken, the official body of First Church should be apprised of this discontent. A committee was commissioned to draft a formal statement to which 15 names were appended. Their resolution is indicative of the spirit and position of the group:

Rejoicing with you in the work and principles of Congregationalism, and yet feeling that this church is not fulfilling its mission in this community owing to the fact that the divinity of Christ is not taught from its pulpit, and, believing that this is an essential doctrine of Congregationalism and that the lack of such teaching prevents this church from becoming a home for the many who are coming from other churches in our fellowship, we, the undersigned members of this church, feel forced through loyalty to Christ to protest against the present state of affairs.

This action we take with deepest sorrow and in only the kindliest Christian spirit.

This communication is presented in behalf of the following members of this church:

To this document was added an additional statement with a list of 28 more names:

And in behalf of the following, and many others who would be glad to enter the fellowship of this church if the conditions were such as exist in ordinary Congregational bodies:

The next day this document with the lists of names was presented to the pastor and the clerk of the church. At a regular congregational meeting of the church that day the pastor reported that a communication of such import had been received that a special meeting would be called for its consideration.

Those who tendered this document felt there was no hope of reconciling their differences with the others of First Church. Implicit in these records was the belief that the eventual solution to such fundamental disagreements would require separation from First Church to begin a new church organization.

Within days 55 people had signed a document headed, "We the undersigned desire to unite in forming and sustaining a Congregational Church in Long Beach."

Matters developed rapidly and 27 people gathered for a meeting on Wednesday night, January 13, at the home of Mrs. L. P. Frary. There a motion passed that advised "we proceed to take the initial steps for the organization of a Congregational Church, to be given such name as may be chosen later." However, that very night it was agreed that the name of the new church would be "The Plymouth Congregational Church of Long Beach."

This incident was not without a certain premeditation. Two committees had already been elected — one on organization and another on pulpit supply. Thus it was also announced that evening the Odd Fellows Hall would be available as a meeting place for the morning worship service and Sunday school at the rate of a $1.50 per week.

This recommendation was accepted and it was decided that the next Sunday, January 17, the first session of Plymouth Church Sunday School would be held at 9:45 a.m. in the Odd Fellows Hall. The following Wednesday night a prayer meeting took place at the home of Mrs. A. E. Peavy.

At the business meeting that same night, a committee recommended that the new Plymouth Church be organized on Sunday morning, January 31, at eleven o'clock. The records tell us that "this report was received with joy and most heartily adopted."

The pastoral supply committee had also done its homework and recommended the services of Reverend C. P. Dorland be secured as supply minister for an indefinite period. This suggestion was approved.

Meanwhile a communication from First Church dated January 20, 1904 was received which said,

The protest signed by you has been received and considered by the church. We have no reply to offer: it being our policy to answer with silence all such charges, leaving our vindication with the Judge of all the earth.

So long as the question as to our Congregational standing is answered in the affirmative by the Congregational Association we are not disturbed by private opinions to the contrary.

We shall remember with pleasure your earnest labors with us and regret that you found it necessary to withdraw.

This document was signed "on behalf of the church" and it was noted that "your expression of personal regard we cordially reciprocate and we wish you the blessing of God in whatever church name you may prefer."

The first worship service of the Plymouth Church took place in Odd Fellows Hall on Sunday, January 24, and

Reverend Dorland preached to a congregation of 78 persons. The next Sunday the organization worship service took place as planned and the minister preached on the theme, "Membership in the Church of Jesus Christ." Then followed the ritual of organization. The church covenant was read and 70 charter members pledged to support this new venture. This auspicious beginning ended with the celebration of the sacrament of Holy Communion.

Careful records were kept citing full reports of the worship services, prayer meetings and actions taken by this new church body, yet the specific grievances against the First Church that caused the division have not come down to us beyond the charge that "the divinity of Christ is not taught from its pulpit."

Since in today's parlance such a phrase is open to many interpretations, we can only surmise that whatever the grounds might have been, the feelings were so deep the participants felt they could not be resolved by remaining in fellowship.

In the Congregational order it is customary for a newly organized church to be recognized by the association and to be accepted into its fellowship. Thus after preliminary steps had been taken, Plymouth Church invited a council to meet in Long Beach for this purpose on May 8, 1904. Ministers and representatives came from the following churches: Los Angeles First; East Side; Pico Heights; Plymouth; Vernon Avenue; Olivet, Third and Central; Claremont; Ontario; Pasadena First and Lake Avenue; Compton; Whittier and Long Beach First. A number of these churches have since passed from existence or are no longer a part of the U.C.C.

After considerable discussion, the council unanimously adopted the following resolution:

Believing that it would be wise for Congregational interests and the Kingdom of God that another church of our order be established in Long Beach;

Therefore be it resolved that we proceed to the recognition of the Plymouth Congregational Church.

This session concluded with a worship service during which the church was officially recognized and accepted into the Los Angeles Association.

A primary concern during the following weeks was to find a permanent home for this new church. After much research the committee on location found a suitable lot on the southeast corner of Fourth Street and Locust Avenue that could be purchased for $6,000. The good offices of Long Beach Mayor Townsend were sought in hopes of obtaining a lower price. The mayor promised to donate $250 to the project, which added to pledges made by the committee members, made the purchase possible. The congregation now owned a building lot and could proceed with erecting a church structure on it.

Reverend Dorland, who originally had been called as "supply minister for an indefinite period," was now asked to be the pastor in a call issued on April 2 with the offer of $1,200 as an annual salary. The clerk noted in the meeting's minutes, "With such a pastor, a praying church and the help of the Great Father, the future of Plymouth Church seems secure."

These hopes seemed to be realized the following year as new members were attracted to this vibrant congregation. Weekly prayer meetings during the year consistently included the reception of new members into the fellowship. Plymouth Church's first annual meeting, January 4, 1905, consisted of the usual presentation of reports of the preceding year's activities as well as the election of new officers for the following year.

A special service to commemorate the first anniversary celebration, held February 10 in the Masonic Hall which still stands on Pine Avenue, records a sample of the spirit that imbued this new venture:

The members and friends of Plymouth Congregational Church gathered to observe the first anniversary of their organization. Good cheer came on every face, and tempting viands in every hand. The ladies had made elaborate preparation for dinner and full 300 people sat down to tables spread with fine linen, beautifully decorated with roses and carnations and spread with the best that feminine skill could prepare.

When all had eaten and there yet remained twelve baskets full, Pastor Dorland made a brief, but pointed statement, of the work and aims of Plymouth Church.

The growing strength of the church was indicated by the decision to increase the minister's salary to $125 per month and to proceed with the building of a chapel on the lot purchased the year before.

On March 7 ground was broken and on May 17 the new chapel was dedicated. The plans originally had called for an expenditure of $1,400, but as is usually the case with church buildings, this was far below the final cost of $2,118.36.

The enthusiasm of Plymouth Church continued to grow and their numbers were such that by December 1906 they decided to call an assistant pastor. Reverend Ralph B. Larkin accepted the call and began his ministry in the church January 1907. His tenure was short-lived, however, for he resigned in August of the same year to resume his studies. That same year at First Church Reverend Charles

Pease presented his resignation in October, effective January 1908. His resignation was accepted with the understanding that he should remain in office until a new minister was called.

At a regular church service on February 9, 1908 a call was extended to Reverend Shelton Bissell from West Winfield, New York at a salary of $1,500 per annum. This call was accepted and Mr. Bissell assumed the pastorate of First Church without delay.

In 1904, First Church had been represented at the recognition service for Plymouth Church by the pastor and a delegate, but the two churches had pursued their separate ways. This modicum of cordiality had continued between the two bodies but in 1908, under Shelton Bissell's pastorate, a new spirit of Christian fellowship emerged. In June arrangements were made that during the vacation periods of both ministers, the two congregations would worship together in union services — during July in First Church while Mr. Dorland was on vacation and during August in Plymouth Church while Mr. Bissell was on holiday.

The new amicability between the two congregations proceeded and the Plymouth Church's minutes of September note that after the union services had been held that summer "the matter of a proposed union of the two Congregational churches" was discussed. The hope expressed was that "with the changed conditions we might do so at some future date."

The following month this changed attitude was given practical expression when the two congregations issued a joint invitation to the Southern California Conference of Congregational churches to meet in Long Beach during its annual meeting in May 1909. The churches agreed that each body would entertain half of the delegates to the conference and the sessions would alternate between the two churches. Before that meeting took place, Reverend Dorland submitted his resignation, effective April 30, from the pulpit of Plymouth Church to accept a call to become the superintendent of the Southern California Conference.

This resignation was reckoned as "a thunderbolt out of a clear sky." However after several meetings and much discussion, it was recognized that the call to a wider field of responsibility was an honor and the church should accede to his request. Reluctantly, the congregation accepted the resignation and a resolution of appreciation was drafted thanking Mr. and Mrs. Dorland for their valued ministry during the infancy and youth of this growing congregation.

A pastoral committee was appointed and on June 16 a call was extended to Reverend Henry Kendall Booth of Berkeley to become the new pastor of Plymouth Church. The records note that Mr. Booth's acceptance to begin July 1 caused "a prayer of thanksgiving from hundreds of hearts."

The new pastorate started propitiously. During Mr. Booth's first month of ministry he received a letter from Reverend Bissell of First Church suggesting once again union services be held that summer. This invitation was accepted and when the services were held, both congregations celebrated their new spirit of unity and Christian fellowship.

3.

United Again

The spirit of unity was expressed in a September 1909 letter to Plymouth Church from the First Congregational Church which said:

At a largely attended and representative meeting... the following resolutions were heartily and unanimously adopted and are submitted to you for your action:

- *WHEREAS – we believe it to be a self-evident proposition that two churches of the same denomination are justified in maintaining separate and independent organizations in close proximity to each other ONLY when such extraordinary and irreconcilable conditions exist that each church may do more efficient work for Christianity by laboring alone than by laboring in union; and*

- *WHEREAS – we believe that whatever the conditions which once prevailed, at present we are not warranted in assuming that insuperable barriers still divide these two Congregational churches; and*
- *WHEREAS – we believe, in view of altered circumstances, that it is morally right and economically expedient to bring about a union to the end that more aggressive and telling work along Christian lines be effected, Congregational fellowship as a harmonizing factor be demonstrated and a brighter future for our denomination in Long Beach be assured; and we believe, finally, that no denomination is better fitted constitutionally to achieve a work of reconciliation and just compromise than a Congregational, enjoying the right, as it does, to modify its articles of faith, regulate its business policy and direct its line of conduct in the interest of a constituency different from one another quite often in opinions on matters intellectual, ethical or theological; therefore, be it*
- *RESOLVED – that we, the members of the First Congregational Church of Long Beach, California do heartily put ourselves on record as favoring organic union between these two bodies, on any basis which may prove mutually acceptable, and*
- *RESOLVED – that to this end we cordially invite the pastor and board of trustees of Plymouth Church to meet as soon as possible with our pastor and the committee of five already chosen from First Church and draw up a PLAN OF UNION to be later submitted to both churches for separate action.*

This overture was well received by the Plymouth congregation and a committee headed by their pastor was appointed to pursue the matter immediately. Although there was no report on the issue presented to the annual meeting of First Church held January 5, 1910, a few weeks later a special meeting of Plymouth Church was called, chaired by Reverend Booth, to hear the joint committee's report on church union, which said:

We, the members of the committee appointed by your respective bodies to confer regarding the advisability of a union of the two, do hereby report that we have unanimously agreed that the interests of the two congregations and the cause of Christianity in this city will be best conserved by the consolidation of the two churches according to the terms of the following agreement:

- *That the united congregations should be known as THE CONGREGATIONAL CHURCH OF LONG BEACH;*
- *That the selection of officers be left to the united congregations;*
- *The property of both churches as they now stand become the property of the united church, together with the debts of each;*
- *That, as a temporary arrangement, the morning service be held in the Plymouth Church building and the evening service and the Sunday school in the First Church building;*
- *That the creed generally adopted by the Congregational Churches of America be accepted as the creed of the new church;*
- *That Mr. Booth be retained as the pastor of the new church at a salary of $3,000 a year, without the parsonage;*
- *That the two congregations meet, each in its respective place of worship, on Monday January 24, 1910 for the consideration of this report.*

We would respectfully urge the thoughtful and favorable consideration of this agreement upon the members of both churches, believing, as we do, that its adoption would be for the lasting benefit of both.

After some discussion the question was put to a vote and passed. Although effort had been made to obtain a unanimous agreement on uniting the two churches, of the 104 people voting there were still six dissenting votes — indicating that the attitudes which had caused the original break were not totally eradicated.

A month later the first business meeting of the new Congregational Church of Long Beach was held where a set of bylaws was adopted and officers for the united church were elected. The proceedings of this meeting also record letters of dismissal being given to a number of people, including Reverend Bissell, the man who had issued the invitation to his successor to hold summer union services.

During these negotiations it had been recognized by all the participants that at this stage the united church would not be able to support two ministers. Accepting that fact, Shelton Bissell resigned as pastor of First Church in order to make possible the union and graciously yielded his position to Mr. Booth. This act of exemplary Christian servanthood must be commended for without this sacrificial action the union would not have been possible. The church in Long Beach stands in debt to him.

Ten years later, on July 6, 1919, when Dr. Booth preached a sermon in commemoration of his decade as pastor of First Church he paid a well-deserved tribute to Shelton Bissell:

It is to Rev. Mr. Bissell that the credit belongs for the movement toward church union. I have been privileged to look over some of his correspondence and it is evident that Mr. Bissell felt that the condition that existed was not the thing that should exist any longer and so he made several tentative plans toward a union of the two churches... That united church has been in existence since that time and the old animosities and the old difficulties and the old cleavages have practically disappeared... It was one of the chiefest joys of my ministry when the two Congregational churches forgot their old animosities and their old bitterness and united in one church.

The reunited church immediately showed signs of vitality and growth. New members were received into the fellowship with great regularity. The agreement to alternate services and meetings between the two church buildings was carefully followed for several months, but since this practice was seen to involve unnecessary difficulties a meeting was called on September 2 to hear the recommendation of an advisory committee and the board of trustees that all services from that time forward be held "in the church building at Third and Cedar Streets."

This was unanimously agreed to as well as the proviso which read "with the understanding that this is only a temporary arrangement looking to the future disposition of both buildings as soon as it seems advisable."

With membership on a steady rise, the building at Third and Cedar was perceived to be inadequate for the growing congregation. Not only were names of perspective new members accepted at virtually each mid-week service, but the rolls were kept current because periodically those who were inactive were placed on a "retired list."

The church was reaching out to the surrounding neighborhood and beyond. In March 1911 they accepted a recommendation of the missionary committee to "adopt" a new church being started in Oneonta Park "until such a time as it could walk alone." This became a foretaste of the missionary outreach of the church for which it has always been noted.

After Reverend Booth had served the reunited church for two years it was decided to call an ecclesiastical council on February 26, 1912 to install him as permanent pastor. In June of that year the church voted to hold all future services in the building at Third and Cedar and the proposal was set forth to raise a new building on that site capable of seating 1,000 or so people which could be subsequently enlarged. Cost estimates ranged from $30,000 to $35,000 and a committee was appointed to "get plans from some architect...and report same to the church at a later date."

By October the committee could submit plans drawn up by H. M. Patterson of Los Angeles and these were formally adopted by the church. Both the congregartion and the community were canvassed for funds. At a business meeting on June 11, 1913 the church was informed that $22,420 had been raised for the building fund. To this was added the anticipated income of $20,000 from selling the Plymouth Church property. Mr. and Mrs. Jotham Bixby pledged a $25,000 contribution toward the new building — and so it seems fitting that their portraits continue to hang in the Koinonia Room of the church.

With this funding at hand the committee was authorized to proceed with erecting a new church structure whose cost was not to exceed $85,000. But when the bids were submitted, the church voted to accept C. T. McGrew's proposal of $90,000. Legal papers were drawn up limiting the expenditure for the new building to $100,000 whereupon the architect explained that the cost of painting, decorating and art glass was not included in the given figure.

The old building was sold to the Methodists who moved it to the corner of Hill and Lime. During the construction period the congregation met in the Plymouth Chapel on the corner of Fourth and Locust.

At the ceremony initiating construction, Mr. Jotham Bixby, called the "Father of Long Beach," was honored and presented with an ebony–handled silver trowel inscribed, "Presented to Jotham Bixby by the Congregational Church of Long Beach on the occasion of the cornerstone laying of the church on his 83rd birthday, January 20, 1914."

The service of worship which followed was attended by various civic dignitaries and church officials. The Long Beach Municipal Band furnished the music and Reverend Booth delivered the address. A newspaper account of the event said that through the pastor's efforts "the church has become a strong factor for good in Long Beach" and then went on to list the documents placed in the cornerstone which included "Original Manuscript of the By-laws of the First Congregational Church, March 1888" as well as the "List of Contributors to the Building Fund."

From this point the construction proceeded rapidly. On March 29 the building committee chair announced to the congregation that the cost of the new building, furnished, would be $130,000. Authorization to proceed and carry the work to completion was voted, and the minutes record that "our pastor, Mr. Booth, brought joy to all our hearts by saying that he would stay by us until every dollar of the church debt was paid."

On September 13, 1914, an enthusiastic group gathered at the Plymouth Chapel for Sunday school. They then marched en masse to the new construction site where their regular session was carried on for the first time in the new Sunday school room. The worship service followed in the same room that morning at eleven. Just before the year ended, on December 27, the congregation was able to dedicate the magnificent new sanctuary for worship services.

The newspaper account of the event said "the congregation taxed the seating capacity of the church" and the dedicatory sermon was delivered by Reverend Daniel F. Fox, minister of the First Congregational Church of Pasadena. That evening the church was filled again for a grand organ recital to dedicate the newly installed Hathaway memorial organ. The official church minutes said,

Today crowned with success our efforts as a united church when our beautiful new church was dedicated to the service of our Heavenly Father and his Son Jesus Christ. Careful planning and months of patient toil have gone into the construction of this building, the result being a structure of surpassing beauty combined with all the features necessary for carrying on our work as a Christian church. Our hearts all turned to God in thanksgiving for thus blessing the work of our hands.

The service bulletin also noted that the total cost of the building, including the furnishings and organ, came to $165,000 — considerably higher than the $35,000 estimate that had been proposed in 1912. Fortunately it was not only the estimated costs which escalated during this period — but also membership of the church kept growing during this construction period. In January 1914 there had been 410 members. During that year 101 new members were added to the rolls. Even so the construction of an edifice of this magnitude was a tremendous achievement for a congregation of that size.

From this point on membership grew rapidly. Each week's business meeting tended to record a list of new additions. Easter 1916 saw 52 members received into the church's fellowship — including Sadie Nixon, Mary Lowry Becker and Ruth Lowry Sherritt — still staunch members who helped celebrate the centennial in 1988.

Shortly after the dedication of the new building Mr. Booth inaugurated immensely popular Sunday evening services featuring lectures on the Bible and important issues facing the public in the political or social realm. The fame of these evenings spread and people came from far and near to worship and to share in the inspiration of the lectures.

On February 9, 1917 an era passed for Jotham Bixby, the generous patron of the church, died. Memorial services for him filled the church to overflowing and "bore eloquent testimony to the respect and affection in which he was held in the community and the entire Southland."

The dedication of the great rose window in the west wall of the church sanctuary the next year on March 3 to honor Mr. and Mrs. Jotham Bixby was a fitting memorial to their generous participation in the church life and the support they had brought to the church since first donating the land on which it was built. The window contains four principal medallions to represent the writers of the Gospels plus twelve smaller medallions with appropriate symbols for each of the apostles.

There are two additional rose windows in the church and the presence of these three great circular windows was perhaps the most distinctive feature of the new sanctuary. The east wall window is inscribed in the center with the opening verse of Psalm 148, "Praise the Lord," and has eight medallions of angelic figures holding lilies while in postures of adoration alternating with medallions of geometric design. The window on the north wall consists of medallions of geometric designs. Each window is beautifully framed in wood carved in high relief with flowers and medallions and made of stained glass that had been imported from Germany just before the outbreak of World War I.

The church was beautifully accoutred and worthy of the national reputation it was building.

4.

The Between War Period

When Armistice Day was announced November 11, 1918 ending the World War, a new era was ushered in for the country and the church. Many in the congregation had served in the armed forces during that conflict. The December issue of *The Pilgrim*, the church's publication, listed 87 names of those from the congregation who had served in the armed forces.

These next few years saw many salutary events. In 1987 the *Pilgrim Pines NOW* reported that "The forerunner for Christian camping for Congregationalists in Southern California was a youth conference in 1920 held in the basement of the First Congregational Chuirch of Long Beach, directed by Sarah Bundy."

On June 4, 1919 the Chicago Theological Seminary, at its annual commencement ceremonies, conferred on Henry Kendall Booth the honorary degree of Doctor of Divinity. Later in the same year, on November 30, the beautiful baptismal font and organ chimes were dedicated to the memory of Richard Loynes, a well-known citizen of Long Beach and long-time member of the church.

When Dr. Booth looked back on "Ten years in Long Beach" he mentioned that the membership of the small beach hamlet of Long Beach when he had first come had been 17,000 people. That decade saw the town grow to 56,000 and 875 new members brought into the church's fellowship.

In January the next year the church treasurer announced that the mortgage on the church structure had been reduced to $22,500. The trustees recommended a campaign be launched that spring to discharge the remaining indebtedness. This challenge was accepted and on Easter that year the trustees reported that the entire amount had been raised and the church could now carry on its work free of debt.

The *1920 Yearbook of Congregational Churches* reported that First Congregation Church of Long Beach had the largest gain in membership of any Congregational church in the United States — 217 new members. By 1927 the *Yearbook* credited the church with 1681 members making it the fifth largest Congregational church in the country. Attendance at Sunday school during these years consistently was over 800 persons.

When the union of the two churches took place, in deference to the feelings of both groups, it was decided that neither name would be attached to the new congregation. The united church would simply be called "The

Congregational Church of Long Beach." The union had been so successful through the years that this posture was no longer necessary. *The Pilgrim* of December 14, 1920 announced that the name under which the church was first organized would now be resumed and the official title would be "The First Congregational Church of Long Beach."

The steady growth of the church meant the structure completed in 1914 was no longer adequate and that increased facilities were needed. A building campaign for an additional parish house plus necessary renovations to the existing sanctuary was successfully launched in 1923 and $32,000 raised. Remodeling work began in June 1924 and the ground was broken in August for the new Parish House to the south of the church. *The Pilgrim* of February 8, 1925 carried a picture of the entire new plant which was dedicated the following week. The new structure — a three-story building with an auditorium seating 450 people — was called "Pilgrim Hall" and contained two beautiful stained glass windows depicting the landing of the Pilgrims in America.

On Thanksgiving Day in 1928 a joint service with Temple Israel was held in the First Church sanctuary. Sermons were preached by both Rabbi Harvey Franklin and Dr. Booth. This combined effort was repeated annually with the addition of the Unitarian Church in 1929 and the Roman Catholics in 1934. The early cooperation with Temple Israel was a foretaste of the later development when the congregation of Temple Israel was invited to use the facilities of First Church during their annual High Holy Days.

The twentieth anniversary of Dr. Booth's pastorate was celebrated on July 7, 1929 when he noted in his sermon that in these two decades the city had grown to a size of 150,000 people. The aggregate new members received into the church's fellowship during that period had risen to 3,076. In answer to the question of what factors had brought about such growth, Dr. Booth cited the growth of the city and then continued,

We have been through these years practically the only downtown church of liberal tendencies in Long Beach. We have had through these years a liberal theology — not devoid of evangelical fervor or loyalty to Christ, but a theology which represents the broader tendencies of our church in the country at large. And the result has been through the years that there have come to us members of many other churches than our own who have found themselves more at home in the broader conceptions of Christianity which we have here. There are more people in this church than you have any idea who have never been Congregationalists until they came to Long Beach and who have come into this church largely because of that single factor.

A 1931 issue of *The Pilgrim* reported that the average attendance at the Sunday morning service of worship during 1930 was 934. This church publication was supported from its inception with advertisements placed in it by many business firms in Long Beach. One local restaurant advertised a weekly special turkey Sunday dinner for six months during 1931 that offered chicken noodle soup, celery, radishes, cranberry sauce, roast turkey, vegetables, whipped potatoes, candied sweet potatoes, dressing, Waldorf salad, ice cream, cake, tea, coffee or milk — all for fifty cents.

From 1914 until the early 30s the church's special music was provided by just an organist and a quartet. In 1931 Ray Moremen, who was then the organist, took a year's leave to continue his study in New York. Joseph Clokey came to the church at that time and was the organist when the March 10, 1933 brought a devastating earthquake to Long Beach which caused great damage to the church building — especially the north wall of the sanctuary.

The crisis was met valiantly by the congregation and repair plans initiated, but the church was closed so Mr. Clokey returned to Pomona. During the reconstruction period church services were held at the Concert Hall of the old Civic Auditorium.

By June Pilgrim Hall had been strengthened and passed inspection by the City Building Department so that the church school classes and other small groups could meet there. When the church reopened Barbara Watson served as the organist, again with the help of a quartet providing special music.

The sanctuary was rebuilt and strengthened by July 30 so that services could resume there. The corners, walls and roof lines had been reinforced with concrete and the contractor reported that 260,000 bricks had been relaid, 925,000 pounds of rock, 450,000 pounds of sand, 100,000 pounds of steel and 1,200,000 pounds of concrete had been used to repair the building. In the contractors estimation the building was now practically earthquake proof. The repairs had cost the congregation $32,243 bringing the church's total debt to $78,200 — since the Pilgrim Hall construction debt had not yet been cleared.

Mr. Moremen returned to the church in the fall of 1933 from his studies and at that time started the church on a full music program by initiating both an adult choir and various youth choirs (the junior choir for children in grades 4 to 6, the junior high choir and the senior high choir). He directed the adult and junior choirs while

Helen Davenport led the junior high choir and Barbara
Watson directed the senior high choir. In 1938 Barbara
Watson was appointed as the assistant minister of music.
This team stayed at the church until the fall of 1939, at
which time Russell Wing was appointed minister of music,
a position he filled until 1946.

A special anniversary service was held on June 10, 1934
to commemorate Dr. Booth's 25 years of ministry. Greet-
ings were brought by many outstanding citizens of Long
Beach, including the mayor. Statistics were cited: during
his term Dr. Booth had preached 1,300 sermons, delivered
3,500 lectures and addresses, conducted 500 baptism, 800
weddings and 2,500 funerals.

The next year saw the golden anniversary of the church's
founding. The church had become the fourth largest
Congregational church in the United States with a membership listed at 2,156 members. During his anniversary
sermon Dr. Booth recalled that when the church was first
organized "Long Beach had but recently emerged from a
grazing ground for cattle and sheep with its thousands of
acres" where the two great ranches of Los Alamitos and
Los Cerritos had stood. The city and the church had grown
together.

On June 11, 1939 *The Pilgrim* printed this tribute to the
thirtieth anniversary of Dr. Booth's pastorate:

*On the second Sunday in June 1909 you came to Long Beach as our
pastor. For 30 years our church has been blest by your efforts.*

*Ofttimes, because of proximity to greatness we fail to properly adjust
our perspectives and our vision is perverted. We now take time to stand
away and remind ourselves that we have as our pastor one of the outstanding [persons] of American religious thought today. Week after week,
month after month, year after year, you have poured forth to us your*

thought — so crystal clear, so Christ-like, so fine.... Your philosophy has not been to be great... but you felt you [had] a great task to do... [and] today you have risen high and hold the respect and esteem, not only of the older folk of the church, but of the younger folk as well.

As you being this thirty-first year of Christian service we want you to know that your efforts have been deeply appreciated and we renew our pledge to you of whole-hearted and enthusiastic support. May God guide and prosper you in the coming years and may you be spared to spend many more in continuing your fine work.

He was spared to the church for another three years. During this period Mrs. R. E. Anderson, known to the whole congregation as Pearl, who had served the church school in various capacities was appointed in September 1939 as Director of Christian Education. She was well qualified in training for her new position and served with distinction in this capacity during the remainder of Dr. Booth's pastorate and for the next two pastorates bringing verve and dedication to this important role. When she died in 1976 her dedication to Christian education was memorialized by a scholarship established in her honor.

In May 1941 the church called their first associate pastor — Reverend James A. McDill. The church had been served by various assistant pastors and because of the eminence of Dr. Booth in ecclesiastical circles had been fortunate in having some of the great and famous religious leaders of the day fill the pulpit, including Washington Gladden, Oscar Maurer, Muriel Lester, Robert Freeman, Kirby Page, Sherwood Eddy, Carl S. Patton, Charles S. McFarland, D. Brewer Eddy, Wilfred Grenfel, Douglas Horton, Charles R. Brown and Albert W. Palmer.

One Friday afternoon, October 16, 1942, Dr. Booth was walking in the garden of his home when he suddenly dropped dead of a heart attack. His death was a shock to the whole city. *The Pilgrim* had already gone to press for the coming Sunday listing the titles of Dr. Booth's sermon for the morning and evening services as well as for the following Sunday evening's address.

But the following Sunday *The Pilgrim* instead carried tribute to the eminent Christian scholar and beloved friend and pastor who had served the church faithfully from June 1909 to October 1942. Under the title, "Carry On" this issue said,

We have lost the presence and the physical leadership of our beloved pastor, Dr. Henry Kendall Booth. It is extremely hard to give him up after 33 years of magnificent teaching, preaching and ministry. Words fail us!

He passed away suddenly from heart failure on Friday, October 16th. He is being mourned by the whole city, as well as by his church and his dear friends. The huge crowd that filled the church at the memorial service on Tuesday afternoon paid him great tribute.

Dr. Booth's spirit continues to lead us on! And it always will...

He tosses the blazing torch to us.

We must carry on! And we will.

With the death of this great leader, a long and fruitful chapter in the history of this church came to an end. From a small beginning, the church had grown and was known as one of the country's great Congregational churches.

5.

A Pictorial View

Congregational church and parsonage facing Cedar at Third Street.,
1890.

Margaret Bixby was the church's prime instigator.

(facing page) Church building dedicated in 1902.

Henry Kendall Booth united the two congregations and served the
growing church for 33 years.

Streetcars had come to the corner of Cedar and Third Streets by the time this new sanctuary was dedicated in 1914.

Pilgrim Hall was the site of a vigorous Christian Education program.

Youth services were conducted in Booth Chapel.

(Facing page) The Combined Choirs in 1939.

Stuart LeRoy Anderson (1943-50)

Emerson G. Hangen (1950-68)

Duane L. Day (1969-72)

David M. Reed (1973-86)

Seismic retrofitting of the church required an innovative center-coring process to strengthen the brick structure and make it safe.

John and Billie Pownall led the church's dedicated volunteers who stretched the refurbishing costs of $2.5 million.

The Centennial Christmas celebration was held in the newly rehabilitated church sanctuary replete with Möller organ.

Mary Ellen Kilsby led the church in its centennial year celebrations.

6.

Moving Ahead

It has often been said that institutions are the lengthened shadows of personality. If ever that was true, the First Congregational Church of Long Beach in 1942 was a prime example. However, the people of the church felt that as the tribute to their former leader stated at the time of his death, the church must go on.

War was again fast approaching and Long Beach, as a major naval shipyard, would again undergo all the pressures concomitant with being in the hub of military activity. This stress was added to the tests on their resiliency that losing their pastor brought.

The people of the church rose magnificently to the challenge. Having added Reverend McDill to the staff as associate 16 months before Dr. Booth's death was a great boon. Under his leadership at this time of crisis the church gathered new strength and began to prepare for the future.

A committee was appointed to search for a new senior minister and after months of careful investigation into the qualifications of many ministers, they finally recommended to the congregation that Reverend Stuart LeRoy Anderson who had been pastoring the First Congregational Church of Glendale be called to serve the Long Beach parish. The congregation ratified this decision on January 24, 1943.

A month later Mr. McDill tendered his resignation effective June 1, four days before Mr. Anderson was to take over the pulpit. Reverend Anderson's "Minister's Message" in that Sunday's bulletin expressed his trepidation at assuming the formidable task which he faced.

Naturally it is with a feeling of humility that I assume the leadership of this church, laid down by Dr. Booth last October. As long as this church exists he will be remembered for his great preaching, his social vision, his courage, his Christian discipleship. Mrs. Anderson and I shall always remember the gracious interest of Dr. and Mrs. Booth in our ministry.

As we take up our work it is a comfort to know that we are not expected to fill his shoes — no one could do that. We have brought our own shoes! There is so much to be done by the Christian church these days. I pray that we in this church may measure up to our opportunities.

The new ministry began auspiciously with a fine spirit of response on the part of the congregation to their new young minister. Among his first proposals was a plan for re-organizing the boards and committees of the church — which was a necessary task at this stage of the church's history. This was accepted and immediately put into effect, greatly improving the efficiency and effectiveness of the church's operation. He also suggested there be two identical worship services on Sunday morning—one at 9:30 and the other at 11:00—and this plan was enthusiastically adopted and followed for many years.

In the fall of 1943 a mortgage burning service was held. At last the indebtedness incurred by the building of Pilgrim Hall and the reconstruction necessary after the 1933 earthquake had been liquidated. It was proposed at this time that the church set up a permanent memorial to the memory of Dr. Booth in honor of his long and impressive ministry to the church. The congregation decided to create a chapel on the northwest corner of the parish house where a Christian Endeavor room had been for many years. This small chapel was to include a small organ, stain glass windows depicting the life of Jesus and seating for fifty persons.

The newly completed Henry Kendall Booth chapel was dedicated on June 4, 1944 with six stained glass windows — The Nativity, The Home in Nazareth, The Rich Young Ruler, The Good Samaritan, The Consoler and The Resurrection. A seventh window in the organ room portrays St. Cecilia, the patron saint of musicians and legendary inventor of the organ. The dedicatory address was delivered by Reverend Perry Schrock of Santa Ana, a long-time friend of Dr. Booth's and an outstanding minister of the conference.

Booth Chapel became a great asset to the church providing a place for quiet meditation and prayer, for small weddings and memorial services and for the youth fellowship services, among other activities—becoming a fitting memorial to a great minister whose name is indelibly written into the history of First Church.

Early in 1945 — a year of great transition in Long Beach — special efforts were made to recruit new members to the church. That Easter 85 members joined the church in services attended by 4,000 people which also included 40 baptisms. In May of that year Mr. Anderson was honored by his alma mater, Albion College in Michigan, with the honorary degree of Doctor of Divinity.

When World War II came to the end during this year all of Christendom was made aware of the needs of that war's victims. Officials of the church, recognizing their Christian responsibility in the emergency, began a campaign to raise a special offering of at least $15,000 by World Communion Sunday, October 7. Not only was the goal reached, the congregation went over the top and it was announced that this was the country's first Congregational church to reach its goal — characteristic of the church's response to need.

Another significant contribution to the church that year was made by Miss Ethel Scott who in honor of her mother who had just died installed an elevator in the Parish House — which thereafter gave invaluable service to the elderly and handicapped.

Dr. Anderson, early in his ministry, launched fall and spring adult education programs under the title "The University of Life" which aimed at dealing with various aspects of life which concerned the community. The sessions, usually run by members of the church's staff or other imported experts, ran once a week for four to six evenings and proved valuable assets to the church's life.

With the community recovering from the war effort which had taxed the country's resources and strained the construction trades to their limits, the church once again could turn to consider the necessary renovations needed in the church plant. A Plan of Advance campaign was launched late in 1948 which included providing heating and ventilation of Pilgrim Hall and Booth Chapel, refurbishing Pilgrim Hall, modernizing the nursery, remodeling the church kitchens and dining room and redecorating parts of the main sanctuary. Most of these goals were accomplished during 1949 although some projects were carried over.

When the new year of 1950 was ushered in there was no hint that this was to be Dr. Anderson's last year of ministry at First Church. The church was thriving. The spring University Life programs were well attended. On Easter Sunday alone 3,000 people attended the morning services; 79 members were added to the fellowship and the offering was over $2,500.

Suddenly in *The Pilgrim* of May 14 Dr. Anderson announced his resignation of the pastorate to accept a call to the presidency of the Pacific School of Religion in Berkeley, effective August 1. Since P.S.R. is the oldest theological seminary on the west coast, Dr. Anderson felt he needed to accept the challenge to assist in training young people for Christian ministry.

A pulpit committee was appointed to search for a new minister and the church continued under the capable leadership of Reverend William H. McCance, the associate minister. After a national search, Reverend Emerson G. Hangen from Meriden, Connecticut was invited to the pulpit and he began his ministry in Long Beach in February 1951.

The next year Mr. Hangen participated in the creation of the Long Beach Council of Churches which brought much strength and vitality to church life in Long Beach and eventually grew in strength and influence as one of the important religious organizations in Southern California and in 1954 Mr. Hangen was a delegate from the Congregational Christian Churches to the Assembly of the World Council of Churches meeting in Evanston, Illinois.

October 1953 saw the commissioning service for Robin and Frances Markham—a First Church couple under appointment by the American Board of Commissioners for Foreign Missions to teach industrial arts in a mission school in Angola. This now broadened the outreach of First Church because for many years Mr. and Mrs. Lloyd Lorbeer had been the church's overseas representatives in India.

The organ which had been installed when the church was first built in 1914 had deteriorated through the years until it was only partially playable. In 1955 the congregation voted to proceed with plans for purchasing a new pipe organ and using this opportunity to refurbish the sanctuary. The organ committee settled on a four manual Möller pipe organ with 4,074 pipes—whose weight would require the south wall of the sanctuary be rebuilt. The work began in July 1955 was completed by October the next year.

Dr. Douglas Horton, dean of Harvard Divinity School, preached the rededicatory sermon and the minister of music, Dr. Robert W. Magin was at the console of the great new instrument for the initial organ recital. The chimes were a present of the Temple Israel congregation who continued to conduct their annual High Holy Days services in the sanctuary. Celebrations continued for a week with the next Sunday's Dedication Festival Service televised on Channel 11 and the Long Beach Municipal Band under Charles Payne's conducting participating in a joint concert featuring the new organ.

The response to this new organ contributed to the music committee's decision to actively share this exceptional new instrument with the community and their launching a self-supporting program that brought well-known artists from around the world to a variety of concert programs. Since its dedication, the organ has been used for over 2,000 church services, has been employed many times as a recital and concert instrument, and has brought joy at weddings and solace at funerals.

After Dr. Magin's resignation in 1959, James Weeks was Minister of Music until 1971, when James Bossert took the position as organist, which he held until 1979. Bryan Beavers then became organist and served until his untimely death in 1986. Brian Copple has been the church's organist since that time.

Since 1975 the Möller Opus 8800 has experienced some difficulties. Although a quality pipe organ is a musical instrument of remarkable longevity, by the mid-70s the organ's musical impact had begun to be compromised by mechanical failures. A thorough renovation was inevitable and over a period of several years, as funds permitted, each division of the organ was rebuilt. A trumpet enchamade and zymbelstern were added to the instrument in the church's centennial year and in 1989 the installation of a new five-manual Harris console was projected which would not only provide the organ with the latest in computerized technology but it would also accommodate future expansion of the organ.

In June 1955, repeating a now-familiar church pattern, Mr. Hangen was invited to give the baccalaureate sermon at his alma mater, Albright College in Pennsylvania, on which occasion the college conferred on him the honorary degree of doctor of divinity.

Union talks had been going on for years between officials of the Congregational Christian Churches and the Evangelical and Reformed Church. Both Mr. Anderson and Mr. Hangen had discussed in *The Pilgrim* the issues and problems of merger being addressed at the official levels. In the fall of 1955 the union was announced to be consummated in 1957. Rev. Hangen was a delegate at the uniting synod which met June 27, 1957 in Cleveland, Ohio forming what was to be called the United Church of Christ.

Immediately after the adjournment of the synod, suit was brought against the new denomination by a small, but very determined, group of opponents to the union. As a result, the courts enjoined the officials of the denomination from making further moves toward union until the matters at issue were resolved.

One condition made necessary by this lawsuit was that every church in the denomination had to vote whether or not to join the union. On January 15, 1961 the First Church congregation voted overwhelmingly in favor of the union and the final Uniting Synod took place July that year in Philadelphia when the United Church of Christ was declared an officially recognized body.

When the congregation voted in favor of the union, it reaffirmed the ecumenical stance which had characterized the church from its inception. Since the First Congregational Church of Los Angeles had been in opposition to the union, its consequent separation from the denomination propelled First Church of Long Beach into the leadership vacuum in the Southern California Conference of the United Church of Christ.

Regularly when the Lorbeers were on furlough they came to Long Beach to report on their work in India. Once again in September 1957 Mr. Lloyd Lorbeer filled the pulpit, but this time it was to preach his retirement sermon after 42 years of distinguished mission service.

As was its wont, First Church kept producing people to go into the ministry. Ray Fowler and Bill Moremen, who had grown up in the church, had both gone to seminary and been ordained. Now E. George Hangen, the pastor's son, was ordained to the Christian ministry in 1958 after having served as the church's youth leader during the summer of 1956 while studying at the Yale Divinity School in New Haven. On his ordination he was called to the Countryside Community Church in Omaha as an associate minister.

The church's Diamond Jubilee was set for February 6, 1963 and Dr. Anderson was invited to return and preach at the celebration service. Joining with the many dignitaries commemorating the church's role in the community were Dr. Thomas Trotter, dean of the School of Theology at Claremont who delivered a rededication service; Dr. George Markey, organist at New York's Madison Avenue Presbyterian Church who gave the anniversary recital; and also representatives from Bay Shore Community Church, Los Altos United Church and Crossroads Community Church — all churches in Long Beach which First Church had helped bring into being.

The anniversary was marked by gifts and acknowledgements which included the presentation of a beautiful, embossed scroll from the Board of Supervisors of Los Angeles with laudatory words and a framed certificate from the Temple Israel of Long Beach celebrating the bonds of fellowship that had marked the relationship between the two congregations and describing the 75 trees planed in Israel by students of Temple Israel Religious School in honor of this anniversary.

Other groups that made use of First Church's facilities included Samoan Congregationalists who had come to this area to work in the navy shipyards. Needing a place to worship, a group of Samoan leaders approached First Church in 1956 to request the use of Pilgrim Hall for their Sunday morning worship services. They used these premises until their congregation flourished to such a point that in October 1967 they were able to move into their new church. In bidding farewell to their First Church hosts, the Samoans put on a program of South Sea Island songs and dances expressing their thanks in Polynesian fashion. Their minister, Reverend Tuiofu Foisia, paid First Church this tribute,

After more than a decade of close association between our churches, I find it difficult to say farewell. Our Samoan Church would not be where it is today without the dedication with which you went about giving us the assistance we needed... Many long years ago we came to you as strangers and were privileged with the use of this fine establishment on good faith alone. And now we have been blessed with a church of our own... [You] took us in when our church was in its state of infancy, and now that we have matured, [we] go to follow in the path of Christians as an independent body... We shall never forget what you have done for us and you will always be in our hearts... The only way we can repay you for the great service you have done us is to be good Christians and follow the example which you have set, hoping for the day when we may be fortunate enough to help others as you have helped us. May God bestow upon your congregation all the blessings in the heavens and although we be separated by distance in the future may we always be united in spirit.

When the Samoans held their first worship service in their new church Dr. Hangen preached the sermon. Choirs from many Samoan churches in Southern

California shared in the celebration as well as 20 church leaders who had traveled from Samoa to participate.

At the church's annual meeting in January Dr. Hangen had informed the congregation that this would be the last time he would conduct this meeting as pastor of the congregation. His resignation was submitted in October effective on December 31 and in 1967's last issue of *The Pilgrim* he wrote:

[I wish] to express my appreciation to all the members of our church whose loyalty and faithfulness have not been found wanting in all these years. Your sense of Christian responsibility, your support of our efforts in all good things and your understanding spirit have made my many years of ministry here a joyful and worthwhile experience. I don't know of a finer congregation anywhere... [I also wish] to acknowledge with deepest appreciation the staff of this church with whom it has been such a privilege to work during these [17] years. These are a group of deeply devoted and dedicated people whose primary aim has always been to serve our church in the finest way possible. They are a team, in which each person has his or her own particular skills, but it is teamwork that counts and I have been proud to count them as my friends and coworkers.

A pulpit committee was selected and the associate minister, Reverend Dwight A. Hoelsher, was asked to serve as interim pastor. Again a national search was launched and Reverend Duane L. Day, the associate conference minister of the Central Atlantic Conference of the United Church of Christ, was asked to fill the pulpit and he agreed to come as of September 1968.

In July 1972 Dr. Day resigned his pastorate and the church asked Dr. Anderson to return as interim minister until a new minister would be chosen. Dr. David M. Reed of Arizona was called as senior minister and he agreed to assume the pastorate in July 1973.

When the church celebrated its 90th year in February 1978 Congressman Mark W. Hannaford participated in the ceremony and presented to the church the flag flown over the nation's capitol on the church's anniversary day, February 6. He presented a certificate from the architect of the capital attesting to the authenticity of the flag and then went on to "congratulate First Congregational Church of Long Beach for 90 years of service and express gratitude for the ongoing contributions that this church makes to the social, educational and spiritual needs of all the people of this community."

The mayor also sent words of congratulations "to commend you on your history of service and dedication" and then added, "If your church could be measured by its scope of influence, I am confident your contribution to the City of Long Beach would extend far beyond the perimeter of your immediate area."

Later that year an application was made to include the sanctuary of First Church in the State and Federal Register of Historic Buildings and in due course the church was voted an historic landmark — one of six buildings in Long Beach so designated.

7.

Unto the Least of These

Throughout the hundred years of the church's existence
the character of Long Beach changed from being a sleepy
little village to a dynamic boom town where the oil dis-
covery and the naval shipyards working frenetically
through two world wars had provided employment for
fearless new immigrants. But those years were over and as
the church finished out its first century of existence the
town was now facing the manifold social problems that go
along with high unemployment and displaced persons who
fall on hard times far away from home communities.

And so in the closing years of the century this gathering
together as a community of Christian believers — which is
the essence of being a church — called the First

Congregational Church of Long Beach began to face the growing needs which daily stared them in the face.

From its earliest days the outreach program had been integral to the church's life, so it was not surprising that it continued to rise to the new challenges and become instrumental in many vital programs of outreach expressed to the wider community.

Sometimes individual church members perceived various needs — in the community and farther afield — and became concerned with sharing with each other and with those around them the love of Christ in very concrete ways. Some outreach programs were begun after careful consideration, others came about almost by accident in response to emergencies that called for a helping hand.

From the earliest days of the church it was often the women who spearheaded this spirit of outreach, with the men joining in on the excitement. The development of several church groups originated from a desire for fellowship which was recognized by Dr. Stuart Leroy Anderson who helped organize these circles. Once formed, they proved to be a valuable means for developing strong bonds of friendship as members within these groups worked together and participated in various endeavors inside and outside the church.

Groups like the Friday Nighters were an example of this. Originally they came together as the Junior Dames, but in 1944 it was decided they should go coed and start potluck dinners which were held in the Mayflower Room of Pilgrim Hall. These were the years of World War II and many of the couples were service connected. Some were looking for a temporary church home while others were moving permanently to the area. In the early 1950s, the group had grown so large that they divided into smaller segments of eleven couples each and returned to home meetings.

Programs at the meetings varied from travel talks, music recitals, impromptu drama, book reviews, games, and forums for learning more about the church and the city. From the yearly dues, or by special assessment, this group contributed to church-related projects such as the Summer Day Camp and the Pastor's Pantry.

From the congregants' kitchens came casseroles for the Armed Services "Y" (during, and following the war), as well as cookies for church coffee hours, food for the Friendship Fair and church luncheons, not to mention cakes for ice cream socials. Members also opened their homes to church visitors from other countries and to exchange students. Work projects around the church were often formed as teams wielded paint brushes in Sunday school rooms and the nursery.

Various groups have come together through the years to meet the church's needs. The Firesiders and the Two-By-Two Friendship Club were formed after World War II and many of the members were recent veterans who were just beginning or reentering interrupted careers. Many new parents bonded together at this time as they looked for insights about common struggles. Each new couple was a welcome addition and the church membership surged during these years.

In these small groups the church members shared with one another's joy as well as tragedy, learning what it meant to "bear each others' burdens" in Christian love. Other such fellowship groups in the church included the Winthrop Couple's Club, the Revelers Club and the Uniters Friendship Group whose goal was to plan activities that would improve the church and its outreach with projects which included raising support for the American Board of Foreign Missions in various ways and the serving of coffee in the Koinonia Room each Sunday after church. These groups also refurbished the nursery — painting, making drapes and donating various pieces of equipment to keep it functional — and helped with the opening of the Children's Creative Center.

Thus in continuing with the philosophy of giving, not only of money, but of time and talents as well, the church members have been faithful to the theme, expressed by Jotham Bixby in 1888 — service. Throughout the years there have been many sociological changes in the community surrounding the church, and the administration of the church has always tried to be aware of these factors and to meet the needs of the changing community.

The church has consequently demonstrated that the Church of Jesus Christ has an important role to play at the heart of the city. The trend in modern times has been for churches at the center of a city to sell their valuable property and move to the suburbs. First Church has consistently resisted this temptation and maintained its place at the heart of Long Beach in the belief that there a unique ministry can and should be rendered.

The ministries to the children of the community are an excellent example of the spirit of the church carried into the community. Under the guidance of Dr. Day, Dorothy Baker and the the Social Action Committee, First Congregational began the Summer Day Camp in 1970 as a non-sectarian program of love, concern and care which would be conducive to the personal growth of the children who lived in the downtown area of Long Beach.

The first year's program reached some 80 children, mostly Caucasian, who attend the weekly program. By

1982, the average attendance had grown to about 300, with children from Hispanic, Black, Asian and Caucasian families coming to the Saturday sessions which included a balanced program of nutrition (breakfast and lunch), creative crafts, recreation, field trips as well as educational tutoring in reading and arithmetic.

As the efforts were evaluated after the first Summer Day Camp, it was obvious that the church needed to keep in contact with these families they had only begun to help — thus the Saturday Program came into being. For many years an average of 80 children attended on Saturdays, with events programed from nine in the morning until two in the afternoon. When Pilgrim Hall was torn down, the program moved to the church basement and the schedule was shortened so the day's events ended at noon.

The children were again fed both breakfast and lunch and the events scheduled were generally the same type as in the Summer Day Camp: arts and crafts plus reading and arithmetic tutoring with an occasional field trip to the library and other points of interest. The difference these programs have made in the lives of the children who come to them could never be calculated this side of heaven. Both the Summer Day Camp and the Saturday Program (which the present children call "Saturday church") have given hundreds of children, as well as their families, a place to turn to when help is needed.

The meal programs have helped provide a proper diet which obviously bettered the physical well-being of many of the children — thus helping to improve their behavior and performance in school. Beyond this, these courses taught hundreds of children the ethics and the rules of society which have enabled them to perform better, not only in school, but at home and in the church. Even though most of these children live in high-crime areas, as far as anyone involved in the program has learned, throughout the years there has only been one family where a child got in trouble with the law.

Many children from marginalized families, living far below the poverty level, have been helped to integrate into society and become better citizens of the world in response to this caring program. Many who have come to the program with a low self-image, through their successes and achievements here have developed a sense of worth, to the point that a number of them have gone on to college and to various professions becoming nurses, teachers and psychologists. One has even been ordained a minister of the Gospel.

The summer of 1989 will be the 20th anniversary for the Summer Day Camp and it is hoped as this milestone will be celebrated, many of the former teachers will be on hand to share memories with those now-grown children and their parents who have passed through the programs whose aim was to show what it meant for Christians to be "Love In Action." This outreach to the community has provided many blessings for all who have participated, whether in teaching, meal preparation, or in coming to learn. In the process the First Congregational Church of Long Beach has gotten the reputation among the wider community as a place where people care.

A shorter-lived program, the Children's Creative Center, was designed to meet the needs of growing, inquisitive children as well as working parents. The doors were opened to the Creative Center on February 24, 1969 as a nondenominational learning center and it was designed to help children explore the world around them.

The Center was licensed for 40 children from ages two to five years, and was a fully accredited day nursery sponsored by the church to meet the needs of preschool children of working and nonworking mothers in the downtown area. It was organized as a separate nonprofit entity with its own governing board and it has been another evidence of the church's outreach to the community throughout its history. The Center was open from seven in the morning until five-thirty in the afternoon, Monday through Friday and in an attempt to reach all economic levels, the cost of the services was based on a sliding scale depending on the parents' ability to pay. The Center was supplemented by a scholarship fund.

The goal of the Center was to care for young children of all religious and cultural backgrounds in an atmosphere of love and concern. The planned curriculum was not just "baby sitting," but was designed to be an aid in educational development of the children. Again it was the aim to give the children a better self-image and a higher concept of their self-worth in order to help the children strive to utilize their potential more fully. The aim of the Center was to help the children as well as their working or nonworking parents who wanted to take advantage of the Center's services.

Through this type of programming, the children experienced a greater sense of self-esteem plus ownership in their community, as well as a strengthened desire to strive to improve their situation in life. An additional means of helping these children came through the establishment of the Family Night—which was a weekly program that ran during the first decade of the Creative Children's Center. One night a week parents were invited to programs that centered on many useful topics such as,

"What the Family Needs to Eat," or "How to Get the Most from your Shopping Dollar."

There were visits from local paramedics, who showed parents what they do, and gave quick courses in first aid. In addition, there were several community organizations which came and gave talks relative to the availability of their programs such as a local ballet group and the International Children's Choir. Sometimes the children would put on a play for their parents. A good time was had by all who attended these family nights.

Other advantages accrued from this program for it provided training opportunities for youth aides. Young people from low-income families, aged 14 to 20, were given the opportunity to serve as assistants to the teaching staff. Several of these aides returned year after year, requesting further experience, and some have gone on the college and become school teachers.

Most of the volunteer teachers were teachers in the public school system who wanted additional experience with children. Some of the teachers were college students and graduate students seeking to broaden their experiences. All teachers were required to have previous experience in working with children before they could participate in the program—which was funded through the generosity of many church members as well as through several community organizations. The Summer Youth Employment Program, and the United States Department of Agriculture have also contributed to various aspects of funding the program.

However, the Center was forced to close its doors on April 11, 1975 after Pilgrim Hall failed to meet earthquake requirements. The congregation decided that the old hall was too costly to repair so it was demolished a few months after the closing of the Center which ultimately resulted in another area of service to the community — the building of Plymouth West, a church-related retirement apartment building adjacent to the church.

The need for such an enterprise had long been apparent. The church had acquired a large plot of land that lay to the west which was used temporarily as parking space. Dr. Duane Day appointed a committee which was mandated to study such a project. In January 1969 the United Church Retirement Homes of Long Beach was established to oversee the construction and management of 196 apartments that would be rented to elderly people of modest income.

The project which cost $4 million to build was financed by National Housing and Urban Development (HUD) money but the edifice is owned and run by the nonprofit corporation formed by the First Congregational Church, the project sponsor. Ground breaking ceremonies were held in May 1972 and following the service in the sanctuary the entire congregation walked to the proposed building site where the ceremony continued with the participation of various dignitaries. Work on the structure began immediately.

In the meantime work on the retirement project, called Plymouth West, proceeded and finally the dedication day came, World Communion Sunday, October 7, 1973 with Dr. Robert V. Moss, president of the United Church of Christ, giving the sermon dedicating this important contribution of the church to the life of the city.

The 1971 earthquake which had struck the northern reaches of Los Angeles made people self-conscious about how vulnerable large edifices were to those traumas. During 1974 various studies revealed basic weaknesses of the church structures in the even of an earthquake. As was the church's custom, a task force was appointed to study the situation and finally a church meeting was called, June 15, 1975, to vote on a resolution which provided:

That Pilgrim Hall be razed and the land on which it now stands, along with the present playground and parking space, be redeveloped as an informal outdoor center, and that program elements of this church presently housed in Pilgrim Hall be provided for within the present sanctuary building or alternative locations.

This resolution was the result of the task force study as well as those made by civic officials and their consequent condemnation of the Pilgrim Hall building as an "excessive earthquake hazard." Demolition began the following year. Projected plans included a courtyard street level entry to the sanctuary, a play yard for youth and children's activities and a parking lot. The city officials also found structural weaknesses in the main sanctuary building as well — not as serious as those in Pilgrim Hall but critical enough to require bringing the building up to earthquake standards.

By the end of 1976 Pilgrim Hall was gone and the renovation of the lot it had occupied was begun but the necessary repair to the sanctuary still had not been decided. This major problem could not be ignored for it was imperative to bring the main sanctuary building up to earthquake standards if the church was to be able to use the sanctuary.

After considering many different approaches to the problem, the responsible church leaders resolved to strengthen the present historic building instead of demolishing and rebuilding. There were various possible methods for renovation, but finally a long range master plan was inaugurated and at the annual meeting of the church in January 1984 it was announced that almost a third of the $3 million needed was at hand.

In February "push tests" were made in different areas of the building to discover how much stress the brick walls could absorb before movement occurred. The data uncovered was then used in a formula to determine how to cure the building's seismic hazard problems. The next month Long Beach city officials approved giving the church four years to accomplish the necessary refurbishing.

Later that year tests of a new strengthening process were conducted on an unreinforced Pine Avenue building which was scheduled to be torn down. Before its demolition the building was reinforced under the direction of the National Service Foundation so lessons learned from this test could be utilized in strengthening the walls of the First Church sanctuary, among other buildings.

These tests were successful and the method developed was called the "center-core" system. Instead of ripping away a building's exterior or interior to install steel reinforcing columns and beams, the center-core technique used a diamond-bit coring drill to bore four-inch holes in each wall from top to bottom at intervals of about six feet. A length of steel rod is then placed in the hole and a liquid mass of polyester and sand is poured into the hole. When this combination hardens it forms a column that reinforces the brick wall.

The poured-in mix also percolates through the cavities in the wall to fill pockets untouched by cement or grout, stitching the bricks together and giving the wall added strength. First Church would be a pioneer in the use of this new technology — a system which will undoubtedly be used in many other structures.

The city's Building and Safety Department approved the new technology for reinforcing the building in June 1985 and in September the church engaged the services of an architect to begin the project resisting any temptation to relocate away from the heart of the city and leave the myriad problems involved with being in the center of where the action continues to be.

The church was especially blessed to have one of its long-time members, John Pownall, retire from his position of being a project manager in time to volunteer to oversee this seismic rehabilitation program. Not only did this reduce the total cost for the church — one estimate put the figure at approximately 20 percent of the multimillion dollar budget — but having this kind of concerned and experienced manager face the inevitable emergencies and solve the unforeseeable problems that arose during the 15 months of reconstruction was an incalculable boon to the church.

The congregation was gratified to have this project virtually completed in time so that the centennial celebrations — presided over by the church's first woman senior minister, Mary Ellen Kilsby, who began her ministry in the church in February 1988 exactly 100 years after the church's founding Sunday — could enjoy the beautifully outfitted and safely secured surroundings.

In the century of its existence First Congregational Church in Long Beach has been a great asset to the town and has been involved in projects such as setting up the Long Beach Food Bank — a voluntary food program to feed people who were not eligible for other forms of assistance. Through the years the church community has contributed money and volunteers to aid in the Food Bank and making contacts that resulted in the local markets contributing over a thousand pounds of surplus food daily. Each month 1,300 people were given food assistance. Concurrently the church promoted bringing the Farmer's Market back to Long Beach since the open market on Cedar Avenue had been closed years before to make way for rebuilding the civic center.

Since the demolition of Pilgrim Hall provided a large parking area suitable for such a venture, under the auspices of the Southern California Ecumenical Council's Interfaith Hunger Coalition, a farmer's market was initiated in 1980 on Friday mornings in the parking lot. Subsequently the city agreed to accommodate this thriving market by closing Cedar Avenue between Broadway and Third so that people, who come from far and near, could purchase fresh fruits, vegetables and other foods directly from the farmers.

This compelemented another program started in 1971 when the church agreed to become Long Beach's first site for its Meals On Wheels program. Thanks to the energetic support of many generous contributors and dedicated volunteers who load and deliver these meals gratis, this program has continued to flourish until today this self-supporting project delivers 400 hot meals daily to 200 people in the neighborhood who are elderly or handicapped.

Another outreach ministry of the church began in 1979 when they joined with the Beach-Wood Chapter of the California Association for Physically Handicapped to launch plans for building barrier-free housing for the physically handicapped. Finally on March 20, 1983 ground breaking occurred at the corner of Fifth and Magnolia for the Beach-Wood Project which would, with HUD financing, provide 97 apartments specifically designed to meet the unique needs for accessibility of the physically handicapped person.

To care for the needs of the hungry of the world, the church began to participate in the Church World Service's Hunger Walk program and each year First Church became the starting point for the Long Beach Hunger Run and Walk which raised considerable funds for this international hunger program. They also participated in the ecumenical Worldwide Communion Sunday and raised money to support the Downtown Mission, the Lydia House, the YWCA Women Shelter, local food banks, the Sarah Center for Child Abuse, the Abused Women's Center and the Rescue Mission.

Throughout its century of history, First Congregational Church of Long Beach has been committed to outreach both inside and outside the community of faith. When the church ceases to be concerned about people and their needs, the church will cease to exist. Time and space have prevented further writing about the many programs available to those who come in contact with First Church, but it will always be remembered as existing in the "heart" of the city of Long Beach, pumping vitality and love into the rest of the city.

8.

Epilogue

One hundred years! Not a long time from the perspective of world history, but in California church history it is still rare enough to be notable. The little seaside camp meeting site has grown into a major metropolis since 1888. What is now commonplace was undreamed of then. The Little Cerritos Hall on the corner of Third and Cedar has been transformed into a great church organization with hundreds of loyal and devoted members.

First Congregational Church has always taken its Congregational heritage seriously. The Pilgrims came to America to escape persecution for their religious beliefs and find freedom. They established a new denomination on the cornerstone of religious freedom. First Church has always been true to that heritage.

When differences appeared among the members of the church at the beginning of the 20th century, the records indicate little evidence of either the controversy or the bad feelings between those who disagreed. The dissident group went their way amicably to establish a new church and the congregation at the original site continued on.

It was an exercise of religious freedom that the relations between the two groups continued without rancor and on the plane of Christian fellowship. The way was paved so when Plymouth Church called an ecumenically-minded minister to its pastorate, Henry Kendall Booth was able to facilitate the reunion of the two groups, showing another side to Christian freedom — freedom to separate and freedom once again to unite — all in the spirit of Christian fellowship.

Later when the details of the union of the Congregational Christian Churches and the Evangelical and Reformed Church were being worked out, the argument most frequently advanced by opponents to the merger was that it would minimize or even destroy the freedom that Congregationalists had always enjoyed. The experience since the union has proven how unfounded these fears were. The United Church of Christ enjoys the same freedoms today their Congregational forebears possessed.

When through the years there have been threats to civil or religious liberty either on the local plane or in broader arenas, the church has taken a stand in opposition to those dangers. Another mark of the church has been its unwavering stand through the years in favor of social action. This has always been a central concern of the Christian gospel and First Congregational Church has consistently proclaimed and helped to advance the social, economic and political rights of all the people, as well as their religious freedoms.

One of the strong features of the church has been its emphasis on evangelism—not by revivalism or the sawdust trail methods, but by what the late Dr. Horace Bushnell long ago called "Christian Nurture." And it was this aspect that Dr. Booth utilized during this era of church expansion throughout the country to bring many new members into the fellowship of the church and help First Church become one of the largest Congregational churches in the country.

Another strand of evangelistic emphasis at First Church Long Beach was its concern to aid other churches form new congregations. Besides helping to organize other new Congregational churches in the Long Beach area, for many years the church also supported the First Congregational Church of Barstow, especially during the ministry of the Reverend Isaac McRae. Then when Mr. McRae retired from the pastorate Dr. Booth invited him to come to Long Beach as minister of visitation, a post he filled with distinction until his retirement during Dr. Hangen's ministry.

In First Church's emphasis on service to the community, many sociological changes have occurred in the surrounding community which has required the administration to keep abreast of these factors and meet the altering needs of the neighborhood.

Throughout its history this congregation has demonstrated that the church of Jesus Christ has an important role to play at the heart of the city. The trend in modern times has been for churches in the heart of a city to sell their valuable property and move to the suburbs. First Church has consistently resisted this temptation and maintained its place at the heart of Long Beach in the belief that here a unique ministry can and should be rendered.

Ministers of the Church

1888	Rev. A. J. Wells
1889-1893	Rev. R. M. Webster
1893-1899	Rev. Sidney C. Kendall
1899-1907	Rev. Charles Pease*
1904-1909	Rev. Chester P. Dorland*
1909-1942	Dr. Henry Kendall Booth*
1943-1950	Dr. Stuart LeRoy Anderson
1950-1968	Dr. Emerson G. Hangen
1969-1972	Dr. Duane L. Day
1973-1986	Dr. David M. Reed
1988-	Dr. Mary Ellen Kilsby

*Church split into two congregations in 1907 and reunited in 1910.

Church Members
in the
1988 Centennial Year

Altman, John
Anaya, Maria
Anderson, Douglas R.
Anderson, Sherry
Arbo, Carol
Arbo, Peter
Arildsen, Rachel K.
Ashwell, Phyllis
Averill, Robert
Babbitt, Rev. Donald
Babbitt, Dorothy
Bagby, Linda
Bagwell, Julia
Bailey, Judith Church
Bailey, Vivian
Baird, Laurie
Baird, Ted, Jr.
Baker, Dennis
Baker, Dorothy
Baker, Dr. Edwin
Baker, Glenn H.
Baker, Anne
Baker, Janice Ellen
Baker, Ruth Ann
Baker, William I.
Baldwin, Bruce
Baldwin, Frank
Baldwin, Erma
Barbie, Joann
Barman, Mary E.
Barngrover, Pearl
Batty, Alene Ellis
Baughman, Bernice
Becker, Mary
Beistle, Maruene
Beistle, Max

Bellows, Fannie Belle
Bender, Hazel
Bennett, Cy
Bennett, Barbara
Bennett, Jeanna
Berbower, Steven
Berbower, Wanda
Berger, Michele
Bessent, Maybelle
Bessing, Novello
Bigelow, Clinton
Bigelow, Dorothy
Black, Opal
Blockert, Clara
Bode, Lisa
Bodie, AmyBogan, Jean
Bonde, Lois
Bovee, Olivia
Bowman, Agnes
Brach, Jill Marion
Brach, Lori Ann
Braden, Pat
Braden, Cheryl
Brenner, Georgette
Brewer, Carol Noble
Brewster, Teri
Brooks, Joseph T.*
Brooks, Beryl
Brown, Charlotte
Brown, Margaret O.
Brown, Pearl E.
Brunner, Shirley
Burgess, Lucille
Burke, Maxine
Burke, Robert J.*
Burnett, Anna C.

Buros, Daisy Ellen
Burt, Thomasine
Cadwell, John H.
Cadwell, Ralph P
Cadwell, Maxine
Caldwell, James
Carrier, Ada
Caskey, Ken
Cassady, Helen
Castlen, Bill
Castlen, Barbara
Chambers, Steve
Chambers, Heather
Chapin, Dan
Chapin, Pam
Chatam, Samuel
Chatam, Raff
Choate, Ellie
Clark, Harmon*
Clark, Helen
Clark, Martin
Clark, Michelle
Clifton, Alice
Clifton, Nancy
Clifton, Tim
Cobb, Doris
Cody, Colista*
Coffey, Juanita
Cole, Peter
Collett, Andrew
Collett, Helen
Comyns, Edith
Condoretti, Roberto
Condoretti, Julietta
Condoretti, Samuel
Condoretti, Zoraida
Conn, Carolyn
Cooper, John V.
Cooper, Sally
Copple, Deanne
Corral, Erin

Coy, Craig
Coy, Robin
Crabtree, Jeffrey Neil
Crandall, Alice
Crandall, Graham S.
Crandall, Tracy
Crippen, Jack
Crippen, LaVonne
Croll, John
Croll, Gladys
Cruse, Mary
Cushman, Marguerite
Daggett, Bob
Dalglish, Flora
Dalglish, Ruth*
Daniel, Christine
Daniel, Joanne (Price)
Darby, John
Dase, Esther M.
Davis, Dennis
Davis, Don
Davis, Larry
Dean, Mae J.
Deatherage, Dorothy
DeBoer, James
DeBoer, Linda Enwall
DeBruyn, Charles
DeBruyn, Georgette
DeJong, Barbara
DeLoach, Richard
DeLoach, Julie
Dempsey, Richard
Dempsey, Merle
Dempsey, Viola
Diefenbach, Paul
Diefenbach, Louise
Dodd, Charles
Dodd, Angie
Dodd, Mark
Dreisbach, Dorothy
Drouin, Carol

Drury, Phyllis
Dulin, Rex
Dunbar, Robert
Dunn, Marshall E.
Dunn, Marjorie
DuCourtney, Lorraine
Dvorak, Jacquelyn
Dye, Josette
Dye, Shirlee
Eaken, Walter
Elder, Lulu
England, Robert L.
England, Lois
Enloe, Jeannette
Enwall, David
Enwall, Linda
Erskine, Mabel
Fielding, Mary
Fleege, Alma
Floyd, Albert
Ford, Frances
Foster, Pat
Fowler, Rev. Ernest
Fowler, Marje
Fowler, Gertrude
Fox, Harvey David
Frank, Ernest
Franklin, Edward R.
Franklin, Betty
Franklin, Grant
Franklin, John Edward
Freeman, Marjorie*
Friedman, Frederick H.
Friedman, Delores
Furboter, Ethel
Gary, Bettipage
Gay, Gertrude
George, Duane
George, Eva
Gibson, Sue
Goodrich, Charles

Goodrich, Vera
Goodrich, Mark
Goodrich, Michael S.
Goria, Kathryn
Gough, Marly Lynn
Gould, Helen
Grady, James
Graham, Bret
Graham, Clive Jr.
Graham, Josephine*
Graser, Ruth*
Greenlee, Clive W.
Grifall, Audrey
Griffin, Maud*
Griggs, Maxine
Grimes, Patricia
Grissinger, Edward
Guelzow, Nancy
Gury, Eva
Hachiya, Daryl
Halter, Leona
Halter, Robert
Halter, J.J.
Halter, Tracy
Halter, Vern
Halter, Hazel
Hammer, Genevieve
Hangen, Dr. Emerson G.
Hanny, Gail
Hanscom, Nancy
Hardwick, Albert
Harrington, Jan
Harris, Edna
Harrold, Louise
Hartley, Camilla
Heggstrom, Susan
Hennessy, Patti Grifall
Herbst, Agnes
Herman, Edith
Herrick, Keith
Herrick, Marianne Commisso

Herrington, Aaron
Herrington, Maycie
Hinze, Jonathan
Hinze, Marion
Hinze, Stephen J.
Hobbs, Ed
Hobbs, Maggie
Hogue, John
Holliday, Jeannette
Holmblad, Dorothy
Hopkinson, Bernice
Horan, Kathy
Horne, Edith
Howell, Grace
Hufford, Henry
Hufford, Marie
Huggett, Thomas
Huggins, Agnes
Hunsaker, Rob
Hunsaker, Leslie
Hunsaker, Robert M.
Incledon, Margaret
Irish, Lillian
Jackson, Kathee
Jackson, Ruby
Jacobson, Mark
Jacoby, Sue
Jacoby, Margaret
Jewell, Dorothy
Johnson, Clair
Johnson, Helen
Johnson, Grace*
Johnson, Lowell
Johnson, Dorothy
Johnson, Margaret
Johnson, Marion*
Johnson, Mildred*
Jones, Dorothy
Jones, Elsie N.
Jordan, Dan
Joseph, Laverne

Joseph, Virginia
Joseph, Kristen
Joseph, David
Judson, Harold
Judson, Myfanwy (Elizabeth)
Jurney, Helen
Karinen, Judy
Kellar, Charles
Kellar, Bettye
Kellogg, Paul David
Kemis, Helen
Kennann, William
Kennann, Helene
Kent, Buel
Kilsby, Graham
Kilsby, Rev. Mary Ellen
Kitchens, Laura Ann
Kinner, Katherine*
Kiviaho, Marcia
Kniss, Esther
Koerner, Alice
Krieger, Robert
Kuhr, Bobbi
Kupfer, Alice Clifton
La Grange, Jane
La Pierre, Adrian
La Pierre, Gladys
Lambert, Katherine
Lane, Roscoe
Lane, Nancy
Latham, Angela
Latulip, Cynthia
Lauson, Lori
Lawrence, Barbara
Lawrence, William
Lawry, Glover
Leggett, Dr. Laurence
LeRow, Lori
Levy, Irene
Lewis, Sandi
Light, Rev. Shelby

Light, Betsey
Linderman, Lillian
Littlejohn, Paul
Lopp, William
Lopp, Gertrude
Lovitt, Aileen
Lovitt, Dr. Charles William
Lucas, Campbell M.
Lucas, John
Lucas, Malcolm
Ludwig, Robert L.
Ludwig, Margaret
Lundell, Dr. Clarence
Lundell, Ruth
Lyman, Willis T., Jr.
Mack, Jennifer
Mack, Joe
Mack, Carol
Mailman, Leo
Mailman, Rebecca
Mandell, Julia B.
Manley, Neil
Manley, Carolyn
Manley, Paul
Martin, Ruth
Martinez, Priscilla
Masten, Glenn
Masten, Edith
Mathes, Virginia
Mathis, Dan R.
Mathis, Robert
Mathis, Betty
Maxson, Vernon
Maxwell, Laura
May, Christie
McCart, Ruth
McClish, Lois
McConnell, Frances
McCrary, Laura
McCulloch, Maxine
McLain, Irene

McLeod, Elizabeth
McMillan, H. L.
McMillan, Darlene
McMillin, David
McMillin, Marjie
McMillin, David D.
McMullen, Ruth
Melton, Joy
Merritt, Nancy
Meyer, Kay
Millen, Jane
Miller, Barbara
Miller, Ray
Miller, Maria
Miller, Tom
Miller, Karen
Misner, Jean
Mitchell, Richard
Mitchell, Virginia
Moffitt, Particia
Monegan, Emma
Monk, Jani
Moore, Ruth
Moore, Mildred
Morath, Mrs. Eugene A. (Ruth)
Mordhorst, Flora
Morgan, Marion
Morketter, Virginia
Morlock, Allen
Morrow, Glen
Moss, Suzanne (Pearson)
Mossman, Howard
Mossman, Katherine
Mueller, Kathleen
Mueller, Margaret
Murphy, Mike
Murphy, Ward
Murphy, June
Navarro, Richard
Navarro, Maria Anaya
Nelson, Margery

Neuharth, Walter
Neuharth, Irene
Newcomb, Helen
Nichols, Barbara
Nichols, Edward
Nichols, Una
Nielsen, Herluf
Nielsen, Eleanor
Niles, Deborah
Nixon, Sadie Ellen
Noble, Rachel
Nutt, Evan
Nutt, Nan
Nutt, Kevin
Oaks, Everett
Oaks, Beth
Oaks, Larry
Oaks, Rhonda
Oatley, Sally
O'Connor, Wilma
O'Keefe, Kevin
O'Keefe, Melody
Olney, David
Orr, Don
Orth, Bill
Ossen, Virginia
Ostrowski, Sally
Owens, David
Owens, Sarah
Pacheco, Luis
Page, Gail
Pagels, Christopher
Pagels, Holly
Pagels, Gerald
Pagels, Terri
Pagels, PattyPagels, Penny
Paine, Ellen
Palmer, Irene
Pankey, Harriet
Parks, Brett
Parsons, Elaine

Patchett, Nelsie
Patterson, Lloyd
Patterson, Elizabeth
Patterson, Isabel
Paul, Marie
Pauling, Sella
Perrin, Barbara
Perrin, Dr. Joyce
Perry, Kathleen
Perry, Michelle
Peters, Lucille
Peterson, Doris
Petty, Edna
Petty, Jon
Phillips, F. Austin
Phillips, Peggy
Phipps, Sharon Oaks
Pillsbury, Ralph
Plattenberger, Maria
Powell, Ovamae
Pownall, John
Pownall, Billie
Pownall, Gordon
Pratt, Hoover
Presley, William
Prestidge, Debra
Pritchard, Harry
Pritchard, Elva
Quinby, George
Quinby, Virginia
Raguse, Shirley
Ramsay, Doug
Ramsay, Greg
Ramsay, Scott
Ramsay, Linda
Ramsay, Spicer
Ramsay, Della
Ramsay, Hebe
Raymond, Sara
Reed, Cathy
Reed, Dr. David

Reed, Diane
Reed, Michael
Reed, Robin
Reed, Frances
Reid, Ruth (Betty)
Reidy, Marie
Rhines, Randall
Richards, Louis
Riley, Paula
Robinson, Margaret
Rodrigues, Muriel
Rogers, Patricia
Rogers, Sandra
Rose, Lila
Sabol, Margaret
Sa Marion, Yvonne
Sa Marion, Adonis
Scheman, Leon
Schiller, Gertrude
Schlotter, Edward
Schmidt, Kathryn
Schoenfelder, Ken
Schoenfelder, Sara
Schubert, Rose
Scow, Theresa
Sells, Alaine
Severson, Brian
Sexton, Daryl
Shannon, Ida
Shaw, Florence
Shaw, Mary
Shaw, Steven
Shaw, Vickie
Shawler, Don
Shawler, Evie
Sherritt, Ruth
Shidler, Claudine
Shirley, Marilyn
Siegwald, Gordy
Siegwald, Gwen
Simpson, Beatrix

Simpson, Robert
Sipprelle, James
Sipprelle, Joy
Sipprelle, Mary
Skinner, Cheryl
Sites, Raymond
Sites, Wilma
Smith, Harley
Smith, Marion
Smith, Margaret
Smith, Elizabeth
Solomon, Maude
Squier, Muriel
Stacy, Florence (Betty)
Stamps, Joan
Stanley, Mildred
Stanton, Dr. William
Stanton, Virginia
Stark, Larry
Starr, Robert
Steiner, Ethel*
Stepanek, Phil
Stewart, Anita
Stierle, Paul
Still, Raymond
Stohr, Robert
Stoltzner, Beth Ann
Strong, Cassaundra
Swain, Eric
Swain, Robert
Swain, Katherine
Sylvester, Paul
Sylvester, Katherine
Tanigawa, Joy
Tanksley, Rev. Robert
Tanksley, Dorothea
Thomas, Helen I.
Thomas, Helen M.
Thomas, Terry
Thomas, JoAnn
Thompson, Annabel

Threadgill, Evelyn
Tilden, Charles
Tilden, Lela
Tollner, Margaret
Tollner, Margaret G.
Traster, Randy
Trujillo, Javier
Underwood, Janet
Vail, Leland
Valla, Louis
Valla, Adella
Van Arsdel, James
Vance, Julietta
Van Couvering, Ken
Van Couvering, Linda
Van Overeem, Benjamin
Van Overeem, Johan
Van Overeem, Herman
Van Overeem, Marlien
Van Overeem, Cor
Vaughan, Ray
Vaughan, Lucretia
Vaughan, Zella
Verbryck, Grace
Victorson, Irving
Victorson, Janet
Voiles, Anna*
Von Pier, Lisa
Wagoner, Robert
Wagoner, Nora
Wakeham, Barbara
Walker, Dianne
Wallace, Marjorie
Wallace, Barbara
Wallace, John
Wallace, Frances
Walter, Karen
Ward, Henry
Ward, Elizabeth
Ward, Robert
Wardwell, Judith

Warner, Robert
Warner, Frances
Waters, Rachel
Watson, Barbara
Weaver, Charles
Weaver, Georgia
Weaver, Stanley
Weaver, Ruth
Webster, Claire
Weiss, Julie
White, Kevin-Dale
Whitebirch, Wendy Zern
Wickman, Louise
Widders, Cheryl
Wilder, Ronald
Wilder, Betty
Williams, Charlotte
Winchester, Madeline
Winston, Scott
Wise, Charles
Wissler, Stanley
Wissler, Agnes
Wolfe, Joan
Wood, Carlton
Wood, Laurel
Wood, Catherine
Wood, Edwin
Wood, Virginia
Woods, Bruce
Woods, James
Wooledge, Geraldine
Wright, Peter
Wright, Michele
Yamaguchi, Steve
Yandell, Marie
Zern, Richard
Zern, Mary (Bet)
Zern, Rick

*Deceased

Copies of this book may be obtained by contacting
First Congregational Church
United Church of Christ
241 Cedar Avenue
Long Beach, CA 90802-3099
Telephone (213) 436-2256